MICHAEL JORDAN

THE ACHIEVERS

MICHAEL JORDAN

Basketball Skywalker

Thomas R. Raber

 Lerner Publications Company ■ Minneapolis

This book is available in two bindings:
Library binding by Lerner Publications Company
Soft cover by First Avenue Editions
241 First Avenue North
Minneapolis, MN 55401

LIBRARY OF CONGRESS CATALOGING-IN-PUBLICATION DATA

Raber, Thomas R.
    Michael Jordan : basketball skywalker / Thomas R. Raber.
        p.   cm. — (The Achievers)
    Summary: Discusses the childhood, education, basketball career, and personal life of the Chicago Bulls star Michael Jordan.
    ISBN 0-8225-0549-5 (library binding)
    ISBN 0-8225-9625-3 (paperback)
    1. Jordan, Michael, 1963-   —Juvenile literature. 2. Basketball players—United States—Biography—Juvenile literature.
    [1. Jordan, Michael, 1963-   . 2. Basketball players. 3. Afro-Americans—Biography.] I. Title II. Series.
GV884.J67R33   1992   92-8277
                                                          CIP
                                                          AC

Manufactured in the United States of America

1 2 3 4 5 6 97 96 95 94 93 92

Contents

In June 1991, Michael and the Bulls became champions at last.

1
A CHAMPIONSHIP FEELING

Michael Jordan was almost out of breath. He took a seat next to his teammates on the Chicago Bulls bench. Time-out had been called with just a few minutes left in game five of the National Basketball Association championship series.

More than 17,000 people were jammed into The Forum in Los Angeles. They were watching Michael and the Chicago Bulls hang onto a small lead over the hometown Lakers.

Michael tugged at his baggy red-and-black shorts. He pulled at the terry-cloth wristband on his left forearm. He adjusted his sneakers, which were laced, as always, to the second holes from the top. His jersey— number 23—stuck to his body with sweat.

During this game, Michael didn't look much different from how he had looked throughout his seven years as a guard with the Bulls. He was still 6 feet, 6 inches (198 centimeters) tall. He still weighed 198 pounds (90 kilograms). He wore his hair in the usual fashion, shaved close to his head. As always, Michael performed acrobatic moves unequaled by any other basketball player.

But on this night, June 12, 1991, Michael felt different. He was about to accomplish something he had never done during his career in professional basketball. Michael Jordan was finally going to win an NBA championship.

When the final second ticked off the clock, the Bulls had beaten the Lakers 108-101. Michael cried. He leaned his head against the championship trophy — the first the Bulls had ever won — and hugged it.

Michael also hugged his opponent Earvin "Magic" Johnson after the game. Magic and the Los Angeles Lakers were a powerful team. In the previous 12 years, Los Angeles had played in the league championship nine times and had won five NBA titles.

At times the Lakers had double-teamed — assigned two players to guard — Michael. But they couldn't stop him. He averaged 31.1 points for the series and sunk 55.8 percent of his shots.

"Michael...has been remarkable," Magic Johnson said after the final game. "The Bulls just had all the answers."

Bulls coach Phil Jackson shook Michael's hand.

"There has never been anyone like him in basketball," Jackson told reporters. "With him, double-teams are not enough."

An hour later, Michael still had tears in his eyes. His wife, Juanita, sat down next to him. So did his father, James. They rubbed his shoulders and arms. Soon, Michael's mother, Deloris, came up and patted his cheek. "I never thought I'd be this emotional," Michael said. "When you [win a championship], well, it's just amazing."

Michael, with Juanita at his side, hugs the NBA trophy.

Michael takes to the air against the Portland Trail Blazers.

Was it possible that Michael Jordan could become even *more* famous? For seven seasons, he had dazzled crowds with his sensational leaping ability. He amazed fans and coaches with spinning and slam dunks. He stole passes with catlike quickness. He passed the ball to teammates without even looking at them. His skill at launching an accurate shot while twisting, turning, and faking in midair left many people shaking their heads in disbelief.

During a break in the championship game action, as Michael walked away from the basket to take some free throws, he casually tossed the ball back over his shoulder. He was 12 feet (3.7 meters) from the basket. But the ball went through the hoop!

How could a player be so accurate? some wondered. How could a player be so inventive? Others were puzzled by Michael's peculiar habit of letting his tongue hang out of his mouth when he played.

Just weeks before the championship game, Michael had been selected the NBA's Most Valuable Player for the second time. He had also won his fifth straight league scoring championship. After the play-offs, Michael was named Most Valuable Player of the championship series.

"There has never been an athlete like him before," said Larry Bird of the Boston Celtics. "On a scale of 1 to 10, with the rest of the superstars an 8, he's a 10." Magic Johnson agreed: "Really, there's Michael and then there's everybody else."

Wherever Michael Jordan goes, people recognize him and ask for his autograph. Fans and reporters constantly surround Michael, even in foreign countries. Children wear basketball sneakers that bear Michael's name. People who don't ever watch basketball still know Michael from advertisements and television appearances.

Some observers compare Michael to Muhammad

Ali, the boxing champion, or Pelé, the great soccer star. Both Ali and Pelé were known the world over. They were famous not only for their sporting skill but also for their personal style. In the same way, Michael's stardom reaches beyond the game of basketball. How did Michael Jordan become the most famous athlete in the world?

Michael's well-known face helps sell shoes, soft drinks, cereal, and more.

2
GROWTH SPURT

Michael Jordan swipes at the basketball and knocks it loose from his opponent's hand. Players and fans alike hold their breath with anticipation. There's nothing between Michael and the basket. What kind of show is Michael about to give?

Michael grabs the ball and dribbles at full speed past half court. At the free-throw line, his feet leave the floor. He soars toward the basket. Michael's eyes are wide, his tongue is hanging outside his mouth. He seems to be asking himself, "What kind of shot has never been done before?"

Michael shifts the ball from hand to hand. He twists his body until his back is toward the basket. At the final instant, he takes the ball firmly in both hands and jerks his arms backward over his head. SLAM! Michael sends the ball through the hoop.

As a boy in Wilmington, Michael enjoyed Little League baseball.

The crowd roars. Basketball fans everywhere—even the NBA's greatest legends—are dazzled by Michael's abilities. "I don't know if I've ever seen a better basketball player than Michael Jordan," says Jerry West, a member of the Basketball Hall of Fame.

Another Hall of Famer, Julius "Dr. J" Erving, adds his praise. "He flies. He handles the ball. He makes steals. He gambles on defense. He does all the things you need to do to break a game open," Erving says.

"He makes it look so easy," comments Kevin Johnson, a star guard for the Phoenix Suns. "So graceful. Like a ballerina."

Basketball has always come easily to Michael Jordan. He was born on February 17, 1963, in Brooklyn, New York. When Michael was a baby, his family moved to Wilmington, North Carolina. Michael's first basketball net was a trash can. At age five, Michael would dunk balls into the can and pretend he was a basketball player.

Soon, he was enjoying the real game. Michael's father built two basketball goals in the family's backyard. "[Basketball] was pure fun," Michael says. "Something everybody in the neighborhood just loved to do."

Michael liked to watch college and pro basketball when he was growing up. His favorite college team was the North Carolina State Wildcats. Michael also loved playing baseball and football and riding a bike through the woods near his home. The Atlantic Ocean was only about 3 miles (5 kilometers) from the Jordans' house. Sometimes Michael went to the beach with his older brothers Ron and Larry, his older sister Deloris, and his younger sister Roslyn.

Yet, Michael's youth wasn't always easy. At Laney High School in Wilmington, some boys called Michael "bald head" because of his short hair. "I thought I was ugly, and people made fun of me," Michael remembers. "They made fun of my close haircuts during the time that everybody else was growing their hair long into Afros. Guys would rub my head and make me mad.

"Then there were my ears. They stuck out. People made fun of my ears and called me names." Eventually, though, Michael became more popular with his classmates. He enjoyed camping and, for a while, played trumpet in the high school band.

Michael's mother, Deloris, worked in the customer service department at a bank. His father, James, supervised workers at an electric plant. Michael often watched his father work around the house and yard. In doing so, Michael picked up a trait that is familiar to most of his fans. "My father used to stick his tongue out when he worked," Michael said. "I took it up and made it a habit."

Michael credits his parents with teaching him how to succeed. "Very early they taught me right from wrong," he explains. "You always have to focus in life on what you want to achieve."

Despite his parents' important lessons, Michael sometimes made trouble. He squirmed out of doing errands or bribed his brothers and sisters into doing his chores for him. "I sometimes got into trouble because I didn't look for summer jobs," Michael explains. "I didn't obey my parents and didn't do my schoolwork. I clowned around a lot, picking on people and cutting classes."

Michael sometimes struggled in sports, too. Larry often beat Michael in rough games of basketball. Afraid he might not grow tall enough to succeed in the game, Michael sometimes hung from a chin-up bar, trying to stretch himself.

In the ninth grade, at 5 feet, 8 inches (173 cm) tall, Michael dunked a basketball for the first time. By tenth grade, Michael stood 5 feet, 11 inches (180 cm). He tried out for the varsity basketball team but didn't make the squad. The day he was cut, Michael acted strong in front of his friends. But later, "I cried privately," he admits.

From his sophomore to his junior year, Michael worked hard to improve at basketball. He grew 4½ inches (11½ cm) that year and kept growing! Michael made the varsity team and broke all of Laney High's basketball scoring records. He led the Laney Buccaneers to their first conference championship.

Michael was selected as a high school All-American. But he sometimes made mistakes. "I once dribbled [instead of passed] the ball inbounds during a high school championship game, and that cost us the game," he remembers.

In spite of that embarrassing event, many colleges wanted Michael to play basketball for their teams. Michael visited dozens of schools during his senior year. Although he had cheered for North Carolina State while growing up, Michael accepted a scholarship to attend the University of North Carolina at Chapel Hill.

Basketball was very important to Michael, but he also wanted a solid education. "I saw the school as a student, not as an athlete," Michael explains. "The University of North Carolina fit my lifestyle." Michael decided to study geography at college.

The North Carolina Tar Heels were a long-standing power in college basketball. Since the Tar Heels had so many talented players, a lot of people thought Michael would have to sit on the bench a few years before he got a chance to play for the team.

But Michael earned a starting spot with the Tar Heels. By March 1982, freshman Michael Jordan had helped his team reach the National Collegiate Athletic Association (NCAA) championship game. Michael was just 19. He and his teammates were up against a powerful team from Georgetown University.

Michael earned NCAA honors as a North Carolina Tar Heel.

There were 15 seconds left in the game, and Georgetown led by one point. With time running out, Michael launched a shot. He was 18 feet (5.5 m) from the basket. The ball went through the hoop.

North Carolina won the game 63–62, and Michael Jordan was a hero. "At the time, that was the biggest shot of my life," Michael says.

North Carolina
Coach Dean
Smith

During his sophomore season at North Carolina, Michael worked hard to become a more consistent basketball player. He worked with long-time North Carolina Coach Dean Smith at improving his defensive skills. At the end of the 1982–1983 season, Michael was named College Player of the Year by the *Sporting News*.

At the start of his junior year, Michael felt pressure. He was trying hard to live up to his reputation as the best college basketball player in the country. But Michael wasn't relaxed and he didn't play well. Finally, before a game against cross-state rival North Carolina State, Michael shaved his head. He was totally bald! Michael wanted to cut away the past and make a fresh start.

The trick worked. Michael bounced back from his slump to lead the powerful Atlantic Coast Conference in scoring that season. He was named the top player in the NCAA for the second straight year.

Michael enjoyed playing college basketball. He was popular on the North Carolina campus. But Michael was also eager to become a professional basketball player. He wondered whether he should pass up his senior season at North Carolina and enter the NBA draft.

After long talks with his parents and with Coach Smith, Michael decided to turn pro after his junior year. Although Tar Heel fans were disappointed with his decision, Michael was eager to make a name for himself at the professional level.

"It's hard to give up part of your life, like your senior year in college," Michael said. But "I have to do what's best for me."

Michael was the third player chosen in the NBA draft that summer. Rather than return to college, he would become a member of the Chicago Bulls basketball team. Michael was determined to finish his bachelor's degree in geography, though. He knew he could play in the pros and still attend college classes in the summer.

Michael was excited about a pro career. He was also honored to be chosen to represent his country as cocaptain of the United States Olympic basketball team in 1984. During the Summer Games, held in Los Angeles, California, Michael led his team in scoring and steered the United States to an 8-0 record and an Olympic gold medal.

Indiana University Coach Bobby Knight coached the Olympic basketball team that year. "Michael's the best player I've ever seen," Knight exclaimed.

Before the Olympics, the American team had played several practice games against a group of NBA players, including Magic Johnson. When asked to choose the most talented member of the Olympic squad, Johnson did not hesitate. "Michael Jordan," he said. "He's head and shoulders above everyone else."

Laker Magic Johnson, one of basketball's all-time greats, was quick to praise Michael's abilities.

When the Olympic ceremonies were over, Michael headed for his new home in Chicago. He was set to soar against the pros.

The Milwaukee Bucks are no match for Michael as he flies to the basket.

24

3
AIR TIME

Michael Jordan joined the Chicago Bulls only weeks after earning a gold medal in the Olympics. He was used to winning. The Bulls, however, were not a winning basketball team. They had not qualified for the NBA play-offs in three years. In seven of the previous nine seasons, the team had lost more games than it had won.

Michael hoped that he could change Chicago's fortune. "When I came to the Bulls, we started from scratch," Michael says. "I vowed we'd make the play-offs every year."

Michael stuck to his vow. The Bulls qualified for the play-offs in 1985, and Michael scored an average of 28.2 points per game that season. He lead the Bulls in scoring, assists, and steals. He was named NBA Rookie of the Year.

Michael also showed early that he was one of the league's most exciting players. He had not been a flashy player in college. But with the Bulls, Michael often had to carry the team. He had to find new ways to break free for the basket. "In the early days, I built up the personality and creativity of my game," Michael says.

The fans took notice. During Michael's first year, home attendance at Bulls games grew by 87 percent. People also crowded into arenas to see Chicago on the road. It wasn't so much the Bulls that interested basketball fans—it was Michael Jordan.

Few players were so much fun to watch. Opposing fans sometimes even booed their own players for fouling Michael on his way to the basket. A foul would ruin an opportunity to see Michael dunk the basketball!

Sometimes other basketball players would interrupt their own workouts so they could watch Michael practice. They marveled at his ability. "There isn't anything he can't do," said Wes Unseld, a former NBA All-Star. "A lot of guys can dunk the ball, but most guys need the whole court to do the fancy stuff. Jordan can do [all] those things with a few steps."

Basketball was created more than a century ago. The game has evolved from a slow-paced sport of passing and two-handed shooting to a fast-action contest featuring dunking and acrobatic jumps.

Dunking is Michael's specialty.

Julius "Dr. J" Erving brought the game of basketball to new levels in the 1970s.

By the 1970s and 1980s, basketball was filled with many graceful stars. Players such as Julius Erving performed creative moves that no coach could teach them.

But Michael Jordan could do even more. "Nobody has ever played in the air better," said former NBA scoring champion Rick Barry. "He's a once-in-a-lifetime player."

Indeed, Michael seems to "hang in the air" longer than anyone else. "When I'm up in the air, sometimes I feel like I don't ever have to come down," Michael says.

Unfortunately, even Michael must occasionally come back to earth. During the third game of Michael's second professional season, he broke a bone in his foot. He was expected to miss about four weeks of action. But the foot didn't heal as quickly as everyone hoped. Michael missed most of the 1985–1986 season. He watched Bulls games on the bench, sitting next to his crutches.

Michael was miserable. After missing 64 games (more than three-quarters of the season), he was finally allowed back on the court. But team doctors limited his playing time to only seven minutes per half. Gradually, Michael played more and more. By the end of the season, he was playing regularly.

With Michael sitting out much of the year, the Bulls suffered through a 30–52 season and just barely earned a play-off spot. Not surprisingly, the Bulls were eliminated in three straight games by the Boston Celtics—but not before Michael Jordan scored 63 points in one game—a play-off record! "As a defender, it was embarrassing," noted Celtic Bill Walton.

Michael was back. He was hotter than ever.

And Michael had money as well as fame. When he first signed on with the Bulls, he received a multi-million-dollar contract. He could buy sports cars and pickup trucks, first-class suits and shoes. Because he was so tall and slender, Michael sometimes had a hard time finding clothing that fit well. Now he could have his clothes custom-made.

Michael enjoyed his new wealth. But he didn't live grandly. He didn't hire a housekeeper to clean his apartment. He cleaned it himself. And he didn't distance himself from his fans, friends, and neighbors.

One Halloween night, the Bulls were playing on the road. Michael didn't want the neighborhood kids to think he'd forgotten them. So he left a note on the door of his apartment that read: "Dear kids, I'll be back in three days if you want trick or treat. —Michael Jordan."

Michael didn't forget his commitment to his own education either. As planned, he returned to the University of North Carolina for two summers. He finished his college degree in 1986.

Michael felt strong ties to his old school. He sometimes wore a pair of blue shorts under his Bulls uniform to remind him of his old blue-and-white North Carolina colors. "I'm not superstitious," Michael said. "But I do consider them to be my lucky charm."

Michael began to meet famous athletes, politicians, and actors. He traveled to many foreign countries.

Bulls Coach Phil Jackson gives orders from the sidelines.

NBA games are televised in other nations, and people recognized Michael everywhere he went. But despite new faces and new opportunities, Michael liked being with his old friends the best.

"They keep my life straight," Michael said. "They are my roots.... True friendships develop over a period of time. That's why I cherish the friendships I had with people before I became famous."

Michael enjoyed being a star. But, he said, "I never want to forget where I came from."

4
TOP OF THE LINE

Michael charged into the 1986-1987 season as if he were lifting off for a slam dunk. In the opening game, Michael scored 50 points against the New York Knicks. He never looked back.

He went on to score 3,041 points that year—becoming only the second NBA player to score more than 3,000 points in a season. Basketball legend Wilt Chamberlain had accomplished the same feat 24 years earlier.

Michael scored more points that season than his three best teammates combined. In nine straight games, he scored 40 points or more. Two times he scored more than 60 points—again an achievement matched only by Wilt Chamberlain.

Michael also made 236 steals and blocked 125 shots that year. No player had ever made more than 200 steals *and* blocked more than 100 shots in one season.

Wilt Chamberlain's basketball records stood for nearly a quarter of a century before Michael arrived in the NBA.

In fact, Michael blocked more shots than 13 NBA centers—some of the tallest players in the league.

Michael continued to shine in the 1987–1988 season. He won his first NBA Most Valuable Player award and was named Most Valuable Player of the 1988 All-Star game. He was league scoring champion and was selected as the NBA's Defensive Player of the Year. He again recorded more than 200 steals and 100 blocked shots in a season.

Michael followed his MVP year with more sparkling seasons. Each year he made countless shots in the clutch. Each year he came through in dozens of close finishes.

In a 1988–1989 play-off game, the Bulls trailed the

Cleveland Cavaliers with just four seconds left. The Cavaliers assigned four players to cover Michael for the final play. Michael scored the winning basket anyway.

In the following play-off round, the Bulls went up against the Detroit Pistons. Michael made a game-winning basket with three seconds left to play.

"I love the end of [a close] game because it comes down to that one moment when it's all in my hands," Michael said. "No matter what the game is, or who you're playing against, you have to want the ball. The clock, the pressure, you block all that out. All you think about is what you have to do to win."

Michael's skill and winning attitude earned him the league scoring championship in both the 1988-1989 and 1989-1990 seasons. In both years, the Bulls advanced to the NBA's Eastern Conference finals.

In September 1989, Michael married Juanita Vanoy. But marriage wasn't the only thing that had changed Michael's life. His popularity had spread far beyond the basketball court.

Many big companies wanted Michael to help them advertise their products. Michael promoted a line of sneakers for the Nike shoe company. He even helped design the shoes, which were named "Air Jordan."

Michael began promoting soft drinks, breakfast cereal, cars, and more. People who never even watched basketball saw Michael on television.

Although he was making millions of dollars as a basketball star, Michael earned far more money—more than $15 million a year—by endorsing products. Even Michael was astounded by his wealth. "I never imagined I could generate these dollars," he said. "No one could ever have thought about it happening this way."

Yet some people resented all the attention that Michael was getting. The Bulls were a team of 12 players. The entire team was improving each year. But some fans and sportswriters gave Michael Jordan all the credit for the Bulls' success.

Critics said Michael tried to do too much on the court by himself. Some people thought Michael was too flashy, too confident, and too selfish with the basketball. A great player, they said, helps his teammates play well too.

And Michael didn't always get along well with his teammates. Some Bulls didn't like Michael's showmanship. They resented that he appeared in so many TV commercials. Sometimes Michael criticized his teammates harshly in return. He said certain team members didn't work hard during games.

Some opponents didn't like Michael either. The NBA is full of great athletes. But Michael often received more than his share of praise—while the talents of other players were overlooked. Michael has a habit of pumping his fist after scoring a basket.

Michael squares off against Magic Johnson during the 1991 NBA All-Star game.

Some opponents thought Michael's enthusiasm was meant to insult them.

Michael was upset by the jealousy and bad feelings. But he knew that success often comes with a high price tag. "There's always a downside when you're put up on a pedestal," he explained. "Every mistake knocks you off it. You're always a target for people who want to knock you down."

Although many opposing players admitted that Michael had amazing basketball skills, they said the Bulls were a one-man team. Critics were quick to point out that the Bulls had never won an NBA championship.

Michael took the criticism to heart. By the 1990–1991 season, the Bulls were focused on becoming champions. With Coach Jackson's guidance, Michael had learned that the key to a championship trophy was teamwork. As a rookie, he was known mostly for his dashing leaps to the hoop. By 1990 Michael had become a brilliant shooter from the outside. He was also a better defensive player and a better passer.

Michael did not always score the key basket to win games that year. Sometimes, he would set up a teammate for the crucial goal. He sparked his teammates into becoming fine players themselves. "I'd rather score 10 points less a game and win 20 more games a year," Michael explained. "We have players surrounding [me] that make us an effective basketball team."

Coach Jackson added: "Michael can have a bad game and we can still win. That didn't used to be true." Using teamwork, the Bulls played their way into the NBA finals.

Michael was thrilled. "I've been waiting for six years to get to this point," he said. "We're here. We can't let it get away from us."

The Bulls set their sights high during the 1990–1991 season.

When Michael has the basketball,
the defense can't blink.

Michael went into the championship series with high spirits. "All those little doubts you have about yourself, you have to put them aside and think positive," he said. "I am gonna win! I am a winner!"

Michael Jordan was a winner—and so were the Bulls. Chicago surprised the powerful Los Angeles Lakers, defeating them in five games and capturing the championship.

In addition to leading the NBA in scoring and winning the MVP award, Michael was selected to the league all-defensive team for the fourth straight season. But Michael was most proud to be a champion—a team champion. "The stigma of being a one-man team is gone," he said.

The Bulls were charged up going into the 1991-1992 season. They emerged with a 67-15 record for the regular season and stormed through the play-offs. Although a few teams put up a good fight, Michael and the Bulls gunned their way to a second NBA championship in June 1992. Once again, Michael Jordan was named the league's Most Valuable Player.

Michael takes his best shot on the baseball diamond.

5
STAR BILLING

WHACK. A line drive whistles into the outfield at Comiskey Park in Chicago. The batter is a tall fellow wearing a Chicago White Sox shirt and hat.

WHACK. The batter connects again. He sends the ball arching far into left field. The blast travels more than 400 feet (122 m) and lands in the upper deck.

Who is this slugger? He looks like a baseball All-Star. But this is Michael Jordan, the basketball player! He's just having fun away from the basketball court.

"Michael can do anything he sets his mind to," says Bulls teammate Scottie Pippen. "And whatever he does, he looks like he's enjoying himself."

Of course, one of Michael's greatest pleasures comes from playing basketball. In the off-season, Michael works on his game. Often, he joins in pickup games with amateur players. Some pro teams won't let their players compete informally. The teams are afraid the players will be injured. But Michael has a special contract with the Bulls that allows him to play basketball just for fun.

Another sport that Michael likes is golf. He learned the game in college. Michael takes golf lessons and tries to practice driving 100 balls a day. Michael goes to the golf course whenever he can. He uses an indoor, miniature putting green so he can even practice golf at home.

Michael says that preparing to swing a golf club is somewhat like preparing to shoot a free throw. "It's so much of a mind game," he explains. "You can't muscle the game. You have to finesse it."

Michael is a good golfer. Someday he'd like to compete against the top players in golf. "I'd like to turn pro," Michael says. "I'm not saying I'm going to win. I'm going to try."

But family is even more important to Michael than basketball or golf. He and Juanita have two sons, Jeffrey Michael and Marcus James. The Jordans live in a suburb of Chicago. The house has five bedrooms, a pool table, and a hot tub—but no fence around the yard. "I could easily isolate myself from people," Michael explains. "But I don't want to do that. I love people."

Michael and teammate Scottie Pippen enjoy a laugh during a
break in the action.

Friends say that Michael is quiet, but that he has a
quick sense of humor. Close friends call him "Mike"
or "M.J." Michael sometimes cooks candlelight dinners
for his wife. He likes making Italian and French food,
and he is especially proud of his chicken casserole.

Fans can find Michael on the golf course almost as often as the
basketball court.

Now that Michael is one of the most famous and wealthy athletes of all time, he is able to enjoy a privileged life. He doesn't overdo it, though. "I'm not a greedy person," Michael says. "I live very comfortably...but I'm not out to try to get every dollar I can possibly get."

In fact, Michael devotes much of his time to charity work. He sponsors golf tournaments that raise money for important causes. He plays in benefit basketball games. Michael has also set up funds to provide scholarships for deserving students.

"It's fun to be admired and fun to give something back," Michael explains. "I'm always willing to give my time to help set . . . a positive road for kids to follow to achieve dreams and do well in society."

Michael thinks of himself as a big brother to young people. He tries to set a good example. "That is my whole intention," he explains. "Because a lot of kids don't have that in their lives."

Michael's advice to young fans is straightforward. "Learn to know right from wrong. Stay away from drugs and alcohol. Respect your parents and get the best education you can," he says.

Michael took a stand for the underprivileged in October 1991, when the Chicago Bulls were invited to the White House to meet with President George Bush. The president wanted to congratulate the Bulls for winning the 1991 NBA title.

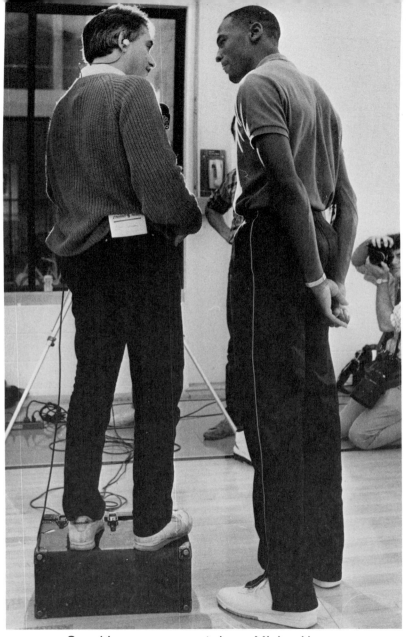

Speaking engagements keep Michael busy.

But Michael chose not to meet the president. He claimed he needed to spend time with his family. But many people believe Michael stayed away from the White House for a different reason. He wanted to show that he disagreed with the United States government. He believed the government should provide more help for poor and minority people. He showed his opinion by not attending the president's party.

Some people believe Michael could do even more to help disadvantaged kids. Many young people want to be like Michael Jordan. They want to wear Chicago Bulls warm-up jackets. They want to own the expensive gym shoes that carry Michael's name. Sometimes fans steal from each other—and hurt each other—just to get a pair of Air Jordan sneakers. If Michael would stop promoting the shoes, some argue, then maybe the violence would stop.

"I don't know about all the violence," Michael says. "I've talked about it. I hate that it's happening. But I don't think I should stop selling the shoes. I've gotten many, many letters from parents who tell me they use the shoes...as incentive.

"They tell their kids, 'Get good grades and stay out of trouble, and we'll see about getting you something.' I want to contribute to that. Goals are important."

Being in the public spotlight and speaking out on social issues can be stressful. Michael makes sure he still has time for his own thoughts. "Everyone has times they want to be by themselves," he says. "I have the same moods [as other people]. I want to be a very positive person in public. When I don't feel that way, I'm alone."

Being alone isn't easy, however. Many people would like Michael's time and attention. "I've given up part of my life," Michael says. "Sometimes I feel more like a possession than a person."

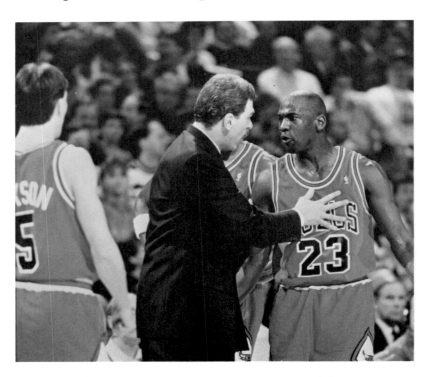

Coach Jackson gives Michael some advice.

Michael doesn't want to disappoint his fans, but he needs to concentrate most on basketball and his family. Since he has become a father, he has tried to make fewer public appearances. He has had to say "no" more often when people ask him to give a speech, promote a product, or attend a charity event.

"The good part [of fame] is being able to stretch myself and . . . help people," Michael says. "The hard part is that every day you've got to be in a good mood, because that is what people expect from you."

As 1991 came to a close, Michael was selected Sportsman of the Year by *Sports Illustrated* magazine and Man of the Year by the *Sporting News*. A best-selling book, *The Jordan Rules*, told about Michael's experiences in pro basketball.

Michael was also chosen to play on the U.S. Olympic basketball team for the second time in his career. Before 1992, only amateur basketball players were allowed to compete in the Olympic Games. But with a recent rule change, Michael and other professional players were invited to join the team for the 1992 Olympic Games in Barcelona, Spain.

Sportswriters sometimes ask Michael when he might retire from basketball. "When I stop having fun, I'll get out," Michael answers. "If I reach my potential, I can retire.

"[But] I don't think I have. I want to continue to improve as a player. That is a challenge in itself.

If I always have a challenge in front of me, then I'm never at the top of my game."

Michael sometimes tires of the media attention, the controversy that surrounds his success, and his exhausting schedule. But it's unlikely that Michael Jordan will soon tire of basketball. "I look forward to playing now more than ever," he says. But no matter what the future holds, Michael Jordan will always be a champion.

MICHAEL JORDAN'S
BASKETBALL STATISTICS

University of North Carolina Tar Heels

YEAR	GAMES	REBOUNDS	POINTS	AVERAGE
1981–82	34	149	460	13.5
1982–83	36	197	721	20.0
1983–84	31	163	607	19.6

Chicago Bulls—Regular Season

YEAR	GAMES	REBOUNDS	ASSISTS	STEALS	BLOCKS	POINTS	AVERAGE
1984–85	82	534	481	196	69	2313	28.2
1985–86	18	64	53	37	21	408	22.7
1986–87	82	430	377	236	125	3041	37.1
1987–88	82	449	485	259	131	2868	35.0
1988–89	81	652	650	234	65	2633	32.5
1989–90	82	565	519	227	54	2753	33.6
1990–91	82	492	453	223	83	2580	31.5
1991–92	80	511	489	182	75	2404	30.1

Chicago Bulls—Play-offs

YEAR	GAMES	REBOUNDS	ASSISTS	STEALS	BLOCKS	POINTS	AVERAGE
1984–85	4	23	34	11	4	117	29.3
1985–86	3	19	17	7	4	131	43.7
1986–87	3	21	18	6	7	107	35.7
1987–88	10	71	47	24	11	363	36.3
1988–89	17	119	130	42	13	591	34.8
1989–90	16	115	109	45	14	587	36.7
1990–91	17	108	142	40	23	529	31.1
1991–92	22	137	127	44	16	759	34.5

ACKNOWLEDGMENTS

Photographs used with permission of John Biever except: pp. 9, 42, Reuters/ Bettmann; pp. 12, 31, 40 (right), Chicago Bulls; p. 14, Wilmington Star-News, Inc; pp. 19, 20, University of North Carolina; p. 23, Photography, Inc.; pp. 28, 34, Philadelphia 76ers; pp. 46, 48, Chicago Sun-Times.

Cover photographs used with permission of John Biever.